OUR FAVORITE CHRISTMAS BOOK

parkland

"The Christmas Tree" by Albert Chevalier Tayler.

Published by Bracken Books
a division of Bestseller Publications Limited,
Princess House, 50 Eastcastle Street,
London W1N 7AP, England.

ISBN 1 85170 190 7

Designed and compiled by DAG Publications Ltd.
Printed and bound in Singapore.

ACKNOWLEDGEMENTS
Illustrations appear by courtesy of the following
institutions, to whom the publishers express their thanks.
The Bridgeman Art Library, London: pages 11 (top),
17, 19, 20, (top), 23, 25, 33 (bottom), 36, 40, 41, 43, back
cover (top right); DAGpix, London: pages 46–9, 56, 57;
Fine Art Photographic Library Ltd, London: pages 2, 16,
20 (bottom), 29, 30 (top), 33 (top); The Image Bank,
New York: pages 6, 42, 44, 53, 58; The National Gallery,
London: pages 8, 15; and Pictor International, London:
pages 11 (bottom), 12, 30 (bottom) 51, 55, 59,
back cover (top left and bottom).

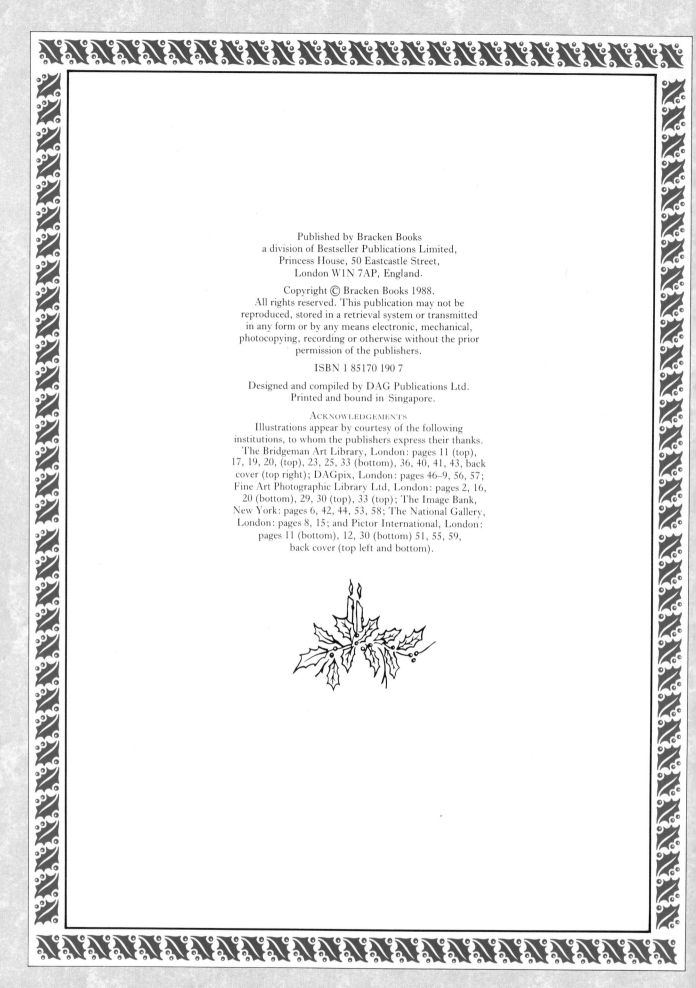

CONTENTS

INTRODUCTION

Christmas: what marvellous images the word conjures up – of feasting and revelry; of the warm hearth and homes brightly decorated, while outside the wind blows flurries of snow past the window pane; of that awesome Nativity nearly two thousand years ago; of goodwill to all mankind; of greetings and gifts and the renewal of friendships; of carol singers in the snow, their lanterns beaming hope and fellowship through the dark, chill night; and of Santa Claus, that wonderful mysterious bringer of gifts to children the world over.

This little book is intended to capture and preserve the traditions and spirit of this season of celebration as expressed by writers over the years, accompanied by colorful illustrations that bring to life the most potent and memorable images of Christmas. Here is an enduring collection of stories, poems, carols and rhymes – the very best of the season's fare. There are extracts from the great classics of Christmas writing including *The Little Fir Tree* by Hans Christian Andersen, *A Visit from Saint Nicholas* by Clement C. Moore and some of the many evocative seasonal scenes from the works of Charles Dickens. Other contributors to this anthology include Alfred, Lord Tennyson, William Shakespeare, Sir Walter Scott, Henry Wadsworth Longfellow and William Wordsworth.

It is to be hoped that this will be a volume to be treasured and enjoyed by all the family every year, each time to savour that very special Christmas spirit. But first: how do we come to regard Christmas as such a special time of year?

Christmas – from the old English "Cristes maesse" (the feast-day of the birth of Christ) is today one of the most important festivals, religious and secular, in the Western world. During the 20th century it has developed into a massive season of celebration, party-giving and shopping for gifts on a gigantic scale, set in a long holiday that merges with that of the New Year. For it is also part of a distinct season of the year, characterized in the Christian world by a sequence of religious observances and celebrations and, more popularly, by much merry-making, entertaining and a traditional spirit of goodwill and charity. The origins of this season are very ancient indeed – older than Christianity.

At the core is, of course, the birthday of Jesus Christ: but in fact the true date remains unknown. Many scholars through the ages have advanced minutely argued theses for this date and that; but no convincing evidence has ever been discovered. Our celebration of the Saviour's birthday is, therefore, symbolic. But why 25 December? The original date for celebrating Christ's Nativity was 6 January, now the feast of Epiphany, the manifestation of Christ to the Magi, when the Three Wise Men (or Kings) visited and recognised the divinity of the Christ child. Indeed, the Armenian Church still celebrates 6 January as Christ's birthday.

The season of Christmas in fact results from the merger of several other,

"The Adoration of the Magi" by Giorgione (*c*.1478–1511).

older festivals with that of the Christians. Indeed, throughout its history, Christianity has 'taken over' older festivals and celebrations as it has triumphed over paganism and other religious cults. It was in Rome that the season of Christmas emerged in a form recognisable today. The Roman year began in January, and between 1st and 5th was held the important festival of the Kalends, hospitality and goodwill being the hallmarks of events intended to set the tone of friendship and well-being for the coming year. It featured merry-making, banqueting and games, and was celebrated with greenery, lights and gifts to children and the poor. But this festival was preceded by the Saturnalia festival of 17 December which gradually became prolonged to the 23rd. This was the jolliest festival of the Roman year, a time when even slaves were given temporary liberty, and there was a mock king or "Lord of Misrule". Even gambling, normally frowned upon, was allowed.

Inevitably, two such close seasons of celebration gradually merged together, aided by the fact that between them lay the festival of Solar Invictus, the "Invincible Sun", on 25 December, the winter solstice according to the Julian calendar (it is now, according to the revised Gregorian calendar, 22 December), and the shortest day of the year.

What better date to celebrate Christ's birthday and, at the same time, oust a major pagan god? The process by which our ancestors settled upon this date for Christmas remains shrouded in the mists of time; but by A.D.336 it is known that 25 December was being celebrated in Rome as Christmas Day.

In 567 the Council of Tours declared the Twelve Days of Christmas, from Christmas Day to Epiphany, a season of festival. The institution spread: the Synod of Mainz established the celebration of Christmas in 813; and it is known to have reached the Norway of King Hakon the Good in the middle of the 10th century. Through the centuries, the religious message of Christmas remained paramount, but the opportunity and licence to make merry were seldom lost. Parties of mummers visited houses performing mime shows; and at New Year young women carried the wassail bowl of spiced ale from door to door singing carols.

The diaries of Samuel Pepys and his contemporaries indicate a period of socializing from Christmas Eve until Epiphany, consciously structured from the holy day of Christmas, through the door to the New Year and ending with the carnival-like festivities of Twelfth Night. Already the traditional fare of turkey, mince pies and plum pudding have made their appearance.

Our modern style of celebrating Christmas emerged during the middle years of the nineteenth century, however, when rising prosperity and better communications fostered the revival of old customs and made them fashionable.

Christmas decorations featuring greenery and the Christmas tree have pagan origins. Evergreen trees and shrubs stand out among the starkly unleaved deciduous trees during winter, and they came to symbolise survival and eternal life. Tree worship was a characteristic of some of the European pagan peoples, and during the dark season of mid-winter the decoration of the home with evergreen garlands and branches was held to keep the devil away. And during the seasonal festivities boughs from fir trees made simple but effective decorations before the coming of modern paper-chains and glass baubles. The holly, or "holy tree", is particularly popular, for it produces its bright red berries about Christmas time.

The custom of decorating the home with greenery and of setting up a small fir tree in the house seems to stem particularly from German and Celtic Europe.

Adam and Eve may also have something to do with the Christmas tree. 24 December is their feast day: popular plays performed in the Middle Ages used fir trees as stage props representing the Garden of Eden. Wafers, symbolising the Host, hung from such trees may be the origin of the cookies, cakes and sweets hung on more modern Christmas trees.

The custom was transferred from Germany to North America by the early settlers; it reached England after the marriage of Prince Albert of Saxe-Coburg to Queen Victoria in 1840, and the Royal adoption of the custom of decorating a fir tree at Christmas soon became fashionable and popular among the rich and upper classes, from which it gradually permeated to the rest of the population.

Christmas cards today reflect the sociability of Christmas, the generous spirit of goodwill that has become traditional to the time of year. They speak to friends, far and near, wishing them well and reminding them that they are not forgotten: for Christmas is a special time for the renewal of old friendships.

During the Middle Ages, wood-engraved prints of religious subjects were circulated, but these probably bear little relationship to the modern Christmas card. The first true Christmas cards are thought to have been produced in Britain in the 1840s, after the introduction of postal services. John C. Horsley is credited with the first Christmas card, which he drew in 1843 for Sir Henry Cole. The print run was one thousand copies. In the United States a New York storekeeper produced his own greetings card, which was, in part at least, an advertisement for his emporium. The fashion took some while to catch on, however; not until the 1870s did they become popular, when Santa Claus began appearing on them.

Santa Claus is today an important figure in our Christmas celebrations. His round of gift delivery, prodigious by any standard, is carried out by the most ancient of transport: a sleigh pulled by reindeer. Always he is unseen; the mystery is preserved, to the delight and wonderment of millions of children the world over.

The name of this most famous and beloved Christmas character is a contraction of Saint Nicholas, a bishop of Myra (or Lycia, in Asia Minor) during the 4th century. Many legends surround his name: once, he restored to life three little boys, who had been killed and pickled and were about to be served up for dinner; another time he saved the daughters of a poor man from prostitution by presenting him with three bags of gold. Now Saint Nicholas is the patron saint of Russia, of pawnbrokers and of clerks.

With several of the other Christmas customs, now regarded as traditional in the West, Santa Claus came to Britain in the middle years of the 19th century from Germany, where it was the custom on Christmas Eve to put small gifts into a stocking to be discovered by the children of the house the next morning.

Our modern image of Santa Claus was formulated during the 19th century. It owes much to the evocative poem by Clement C. Moore reproduced on page 32; here was the definitive Santa, brilliantly described and embracing all the qualities of his ancestry – as well as those we want him to have. All that was required was a pictorial image: and Thomas Nast provided this in the 1860s, with the illustration reproduced on the cover of this book.

A very early Christmas Card from the 1840s.

A Nativity model – the Christmas Crib – in the convent of St Francis at
Greccio in Italy.

THE BIRTH OF CHRIST

Alfred Tennyson

The time draws near the birth of Christ;
   The moon is hid – the night is still;
   The Christmas bells from hill to hill
Answer each other in the mist.

Four voices of four hamlets round,
   From far and near, on mead and
     moor,
   Swell out and fail, as if a door
Were shut between me and the sound.

Each voice four changes on the wind,
   That now dilate and now decrease,
   Peace and good-will, good-will and
     peace,
Peace and good-will to all mankind.

Rise, happy morn! rise, holy morn!
   Draw forth the cheerful day from
     night;
   O Father! touch the east, and light
The light that shone when hope was
     born!

Hark! the herald Angels sing,
Glory to the new-born King,
Peace on earth and mercy mild,
God and sinner reconcil'd.

   Hark! the herald Angels sing,
   Glory to the new-born King.

Joyful all ye nations rise,
Join the triumph of the skies,
With the angelic host proclaim,
Christ is born in Bethlehem.

   Hark! the herald Angels sing,
   Glory to the new-born King.

Christ by highest Heaven ador'd,
Christ the everlasting Lord!
Late in time behold him come,
Offspring of a Virgin's womb.

Hark! the herald Angels sing,
Glory to the new-born King.

Hail the Heaven-born Prince of Peace!
Hail the Sun of Righteousness!
Light and life to all he brings,
Risen with healing in his wings.

   Hark! the herald Angels sing,
   Glory to the new-born King.

Mild he lays his glory by,
Born that man no more may die,
Born to raise the sons of earth,
Born to give them second birth.

   Hark! the herald Angels sing,
   Glory to the new-born King.

The star in the east that guided
the three kings to the infant Jesus.

THE THREE KINGS

Henry Wadsworth Longfellow

Three Kings came riding from far away,
   Melchior and Gaspar and Baltasar;
Three Wise Men out of the East were
   they,
And they traveled by night and they
   slept by day,
    For their guide was a beautiful,
    wonderful star.

The star was so beautiful, large and
   clear,
    That all the other stars of the sky
Became a white mist in the atmosphere;
And by this they knew that the coming
   was near
    Of the Prince foretold in the
    prophecy.

Three caskets they bore on their saddle-
   bows,
    Three caskets of gold with golden
    keys;
Their robes were of crimson silk, with
   rows
Of bells and pomegranates and
   furbelows,
    Their turbans like blossoming
    almond-trees.

And so the Three Kings rode into the
   West,
    Through the dusk of night over hill
    and dell,
And sometimes they nodded with beard
   on breast,
And sometimes talked, as they paused to
   rest,
    With the people they met at some
    wayside well.

"Of the child that is born," said Baltasar,
   "Good people, I pray you, tell us the
   news;
For we in the East have seen his star,
And have ridden fast, and have ridden
   far,
    To find and worship the King of the
    Jews."

And the people answered, "You ask in
   vain;
    We know of no king but Herod the
    Great!"
They thought the Wise Men were men
   insane,
As they spurred their horses across the
   plain
    Like riders in haste who cannot wait.

And when they came to Jerusalem,
   Herod the Great, who had heard this
    thing,
Sent for the Wise Men and questioned
   them;
And said, "Go down unto Bethlehem,
   And bring me tidings of this new
    king."

So they rode away, and the star stood
   still,
    The only one in the gray of morn;
Yes, it stopped, it stood still of its own
   free will,
Right over Bethlehem on the hill,
    The city of David where Christ was
    born.

"The Adoration of the Magi" by Paolo Veronese (1528–88).

And the Three Kings rode through the
    gate and the guard,
        Through the silent street, till their
        horses turned
And neighed as they entered the great
    inn-yard;
But the windows were closed, and the
    doors were barred,
        And only a light in the stable
        burned.

And cradled there in the scented hay,
        In the air made sweet by the breath
        of kine,
The little child in the manger lay,
The Child that would be King one day
        Of a kingdom not human, but
        divine.

His mother, Mary of Nazareth,
    Sat watching beside his place of rest,
Watching the even flow of his breath,
For the joy of life and the terror of death
        Were mingled together in her breast.

They laid their offerings at his feet:
    The gold was their tribute to a King;
The frankincense, with its odor sweet,
Was for the Priest, the Paraclete;
    The myrrh for the body's burying.

And the mother wondered and bowed
    her head,
    And sat as still as a statue of stone;
Her heart was troubled yet comforted,
Remembering what the angel had said
    Of an endless reign and of David's
    throne.

Then the Kings rode out of the city
    gate,
    With a clatter of hoofs in proud
    array;
But they went not back to Herod the
    Great,
For they knew his malice and feared his
    hate,
    And returned to their homes by
    another way.

SO, NOW IS COME OUR JOYFULST FEAST

George Wither

So, now is come our joyfulst feast,
    Let every man be jolly;
Each room with ivy leaves is drest,
    And every post with holly
Though some churls at our mirth repine,
Round your foreheads garlands twine;
Drown sorrow in a cup of wine,
    And let us all be merry.

Now all our neighbours' chimnies smoke,
    And Christmas logs are burning;
Their ovens they with baked meats
    choke,
    And all their spits are turning.
Without the door let sorrow lie;
And if for cold it hap to die,
We'll bury't in a Christmas pie,
    And evermore be merry.

Now every lad is wondrous trim,
    And no man minds his labour;
Our lasses have provided them
    A bag-pipe and a tabor;
Young men and maids, and girls and
    boys,
Give life to one another's joys;
And you anon shall by their noise
    Perceive that they are merry.

Rank misers now do sparing shun;
    Their hall of music soundeth;
And dogs thence with whole shoulders
    run,
    So all things there aboundeth.
The country folks themselves advance
For crowdy-mutton's* come out of
    France;
And Jack shall pipe, and Jill shall dance,
    And all the town be merry.
    *Fiddlers.

Christmas Angels: a Victorian Christmas card.

"Christmas Deliveries"
– a painting by Henry Alken.

CHRISTMAS IN THE OLDEN TIME

Walter Scott

On Christmas-eve the bells were rung;
The damsel donned her kirtle sheen;
The hall was dressed with holly green;
Forth to the wood did merry men go,
To gather in the mistletoe.
Thus opened wide the baron's hall
To vassal, tenant, serf and all;
Power laid his rod of rule aside
And ceremony doffed his pride.
The heir, with roses in his shoes,
That night might village partner choose;
The lord, underogating, share
The vulgar game of "Post and Pair."
All hailed, with uncontrolled delight,
And general voice, the happy night
That to the cottage, as the crown,
Brought tidings of salvation down.

The fire, with well-dried logs supplied,
Went roaring up the chimney wide;
The huge hall-table's oaken face,
Scrubbed till it shone, the day to grace,
Bore then upon its massive board
No mark to part the squire and lord.
Then was brought in the lusty brawn
By old blue-coated serving man;
Then the grim boar's head frowned on high,
Crested with bays and rosemary.

Well can the green-garbed ranger tell
How, when and where the monster fell;
What dogs before his death he tore,
And all the baitings of the boar.
The wassal round, in good brown bowls,
Garnished with ribbons, blithely trowls.
There the huge sirloin reeked; hard by
Plum-porridge stood, and Christmas pye;
Nor failed old Scotland to produce,
At such high-tide, her savory goose.

Then came the merry maskers in,
And carols roared with blithesome din.
If unmelodious was the song,
It was a hearty note, and strong;
Who lists may in their murmuring see
Traces of ancient mystery;
White shirts supplied the masquerade,
And smutted cheeks the visors made;
But O, what maskers richly dight,
Can boast of bosoms half so light!
England was "merry England" when
Old Christmas brought his sports again;
'Twas Christmas broached the mightiest ale,
'Twas Christmas told the merriest tale;
A Christmas gambol oft would cheer
The poor man's heart through half the year.

Wall Street, New York, at Christmas time. A painting from the 19th century.

Christmas morning in the olden time:
a painting by Thomas Falcon Marshall (1818–78).

A classic image of Christmas-time conviviality. "A Merry Christmas" by Frank Dadd from *Pears' Annual* 1907.

"The Sledge Ride" – a painting by Louis Simon Cabaillot.

GOD REST YOU MERRY, GENTLEMEN

God rest you merry, gentlemen,
   Let nothing you dismay,
For Jesus Christ our Saviour
   Was born upon this day,
To save us all from Satan's power
   When we were gone astray.
      O tidings of comfort and joy,
      For Jesus Christ our Saviour was
      born on Christmas day.

In Bethlehem in Jury
   This blessed babe was born,
And laid within a manger
   Upon this blessed morn;
The which his mother Mary
   Nothing did take in scorn.
      O tidings of comfort and joy,
      For Jesus Christ our Saviour was
      born on Christmas day.

From God our Heavenly Father
   A blessed Angel came,
And unto certain Shepherds
   Brought tidings of the same,
How that in Bethlehem was born
   The Son of God by name.
      O tidings of comfort and joy,
      For Jesus Christ our Saviour was
      born on Christmas day.

Fear not, then said the Angel,
   Let nothing you affright,
This day is born a Saviour
   Of virtue, power, and might;
So frequently to vanquish all
   The friends of Satan quite.
      O tidings of comfort and joy,
      For Jesus Christ our Saviour was
      born on Christmas day.

The Shepherds at those tidings
   Rejoiced much in mind,
And left their flocks a feeding
   In tempest, storm, and wind,
And went to Bethlehem straightway,
   This blessed babe to find.
      O tidings of comfort and joy,
      For Jesus Christ our Saviour was
      born on Christmas day.

But when to Bethlehem they came,
   Whereas this infant lay,
They found him in a manger
   Where oxen feed on hay,
His mother Mary kneeling
   Unto the Lord did pray.
      O tidings of comfort and joy,
      For Jesus Christ our Saviour was
      born on Christmas day.

Now to the Lord sing praises,
   All you within this place,
And with true love and brotherhood
   Each other now embrace;
This holy tide of Christmas
   All others doth deface.
      O tidings of comfort and joy,
      For Jesus Christ our Saviour was
      born on Christmas day.

CHRISTMAS EVE AT MR. WARDLE'S

From *The Pickwick Papers*
Charles Dickens

From the center of the ceiling of this kitchen, old Wardle had just suspended with his own hands a huge branch of mistletoe, and this same branch of mistletoe instantaneously gave rise to a scene of general and most delightful struggling and confusion; in the midst of which Mr. Pickwick with a gallantry which would have done honour to a descendant of Lady Trollimglower herself, took the old lady by the hand, led her beneath the mystic branch, and saluted her in all courtesy and decorum. The old lady submitted to this piece of practical politeness with all the dignity which befitted so important and serious a solemnity, but the younger ladies not being so thoroughly imbued with a superstitious veneration of the custom, or imagining that the value of a salute is very much enhanced if it cost a little trouble to obtain it, screamed and struggled, and ran into corners, and threatened and remonstrated, and did everything but leave the room, until some of the less adventurous gentlemen were on the point of desisting, when they all at once found it useless to resist any longer, and submitted to be kissed with a good grace. Mr. Winkle kissed the young lady with the black eyes, and Mr. Snodgrass kissed Emily; and Mr. Weller, not being particular about the form of being under the mistletoe, kissed Emma and the other female servants, just as he caught them. As to the poor relations, they kissed everybody, not even excepting the plainer portion of the young-lady visitors, who, in their excessive confusion, ran right under the mistletoe, directly it was hung up, without knowing it! Wardle stood with his back to the fire, surveying the whole scene, with the utmost satisfaction; and the fat boy took the opportunity of appropriating to his own use, and summarily devouring, a particularly fine mince-pie, that had been carefully put by for somebody else.

Now the screaming had subsided, and faces were in a glow and curls in a tangle, and Mr. Pickwick, after kissing the old lady as before mentioned, was standing under the mistletoe, looking with a very pleased countenance on all that was passing around him, when the young lady with the black eyes, after a little whispering with the other young ladies, made a sudden dart forward, and, putting her arm around Mr. Pickwick's neck, saluted him affectionately on the left cheek; and before Mr. Pickwick distinctly knew what was the matter, he was surrounded by the whole body, and kissed by every one of them.

It was a pleasant thing to see Mr. Pickwick in the centre of the group, now pulled this way, and then that, and first kissed on the chin and then on the nose, and then on the spectacles, and to hear the peals of laughter which were raised on every side; but it was a still more pleasant thing to see Mr. Pickwick, blinded shortly afterwards with a silk-handkerchief, falling up against the wall, and scrambling into corners, and going through all the mysteries of blind-man's buff, with the utmost relish of the game, until at last he caught one of the poor relations; and then had to evade the blind-man himself, which he did with a nimbleness and agility that elicited the admiration and applause of all beholders. The poor relations caught just the people whom they thought would like it; and when the game flagged, got caught themselves. When they were all tired of blind-man's buff, there was a great game at snapdragon, and when fingers enough were burned with that, and all the raisons gone, they sat down by the huge fire of blazing logs to a substantial supper, and a mighty bowl of wassail, something smaller than an ordinary wash-house copper, in which the hot apples were hissing and bubbling with a rich look,

and a jolly sound, that were perfectly irresistible.

"This," said Mr. Pickwick, looking round him, "this is, indeed, comfort."

"Our invariable custom," replied Mr. Wardle. "Everybody sits down with us on Christmas eve, as you see them now – servants and all; and here we wait till the clock strikes twelve, to usher Christmas in, and wile away the time with forfeits and old stories. Trundle, my boy, rake up the fire."

Up flew the bright sparks in myriads as the logs were stirred, and the deep red blaze sent forth a rich glow, that penetrated into the furthest corner of the room, and cast its cheerful tint on every face.

The jollity of a Dickensian Christmas.

THE CHRISTMAS GOOSE AT THE CRATCHITS'

Charles Dickens

YOU might have thought a goose the rarest of all birds; a feathered phenomenon, to which a black swan was a matter of course; and in truth, it was something like it in that house. Mrs Cratchit made the gravy (ready beforehand in a little saucepan) hissing hot; Master Peter mashed the potatoes with incredible vigor; Miss Belinda sweetened up the apple-sauce; Martha dusted the hot plates; Bob took Tiny Tim beside him in a tiny corner, at the table; the two young Cratchits set chairs for everybody, not forgetting themselves, and mounting guard upon their posts, crammed spoons into their mouths, lest they should shriek for goose before their turn came to be helped. At last the dishes were set on, and grace was said. It was succeeded by a breathless pause, as Mrs Cratchit, looking slowly all along the carving knife, prepared to plunge it in the breast; but when she did, and when the long-expected gush of stuffing issued forth, one murmur of delight arose all around the board, and even Tiny Tim, excited by the two young Cratchits, beat on the table with the handle of his knife, and feebly cried hurrah!

There never was such a goose. Bob said he didn't believe there ever was such a goose cooked. Its tenderness and flavor, size and cheapness, were the themes of universal admiration. Eked out by the apple-sauce and mashed potatoes, it was a sufficient dinner for the whole family; indeed, as Mrs. Cratchit said with great delight (surveying one small atom of a bone on the dish), they hadn't ate it all at last! Yet every one had had enough, and the youngest Cratchits in particular were steeped in sage and onion to the eye-brows! But now, the plates being changed by Miss Belinda, Mrs Cratchit left the room alone – too nervous to bear witnesses – to take the pudding up, and bring it in.

Suppose it should not be done enough! Suppose it should break in turning out! Suppose somebody should have got over the wall of the backyard, and stolen it, while they were merry with the goose; a supposition at which the two young Cratchits became livid! All sorts of horrors were supposed.

Hallo! A great deal of steam! The pudding was out of the copper. A smell like a washing-day! That was the cloth. A smell like an eating-house and a pastry cook's next door to each other, with a laundress next door to that! That was the pudding. In half a minute Mrs. Cratchit entered, flushed, but smiling proudly, with the pudding like a speckled cannon-ball, so hard and firm, blazing in half of half-a-quartern of ignited brandy, and bedight with Christmas holly stuck into the top.

Oh, a wonderful pudding! Bob Cratchit said, and calmly too, that he regarded it as the greatest success achieved by Mrs. Cratchit since their marriage. Mrs. Cratchit said that now the weight was off her mind, she would confess she had had her doubts about the quantity of flour. Everybody had something to say about it, but nobody said or

"The Christmas Hamper" by Robert Braithwaite Martineau (1826–69).

thought it was at all a small pudding for so large a family. It would have been flat heresy to do so. Any Cratchit would have blushed to hint at such a thing.

At last the dinner was all done, the cloth was cleared, the hearth swept, and the fire made up. The compound in the jug being tasted and considered perfect, apples and oranges were put upon the table, and a shovelful of chestnuts on the fire. Then all the Cratchit family drew round the hearth, in what Bob Cratchit called a circle, meaning half a one; and at Bob Cratchit's elbow stood the family display of glass – two tumblers, and a custard-cup without a handle.

These held the hot stuff from the jug, however, as well as golden goblets would have done; and Bob served it out with beaming looks, while the chestnuts on the fire sputtered and cracked noisily. Then Bob proposed:

"A merry Christmas to us all, my dears. God bless us!"

Which all the family re-echoed.

"God bless us every one!" said Tiny Tim, the last of all.

A CHRISTMAS DINNER

Charles Dickens

Christmas time! That man must be a misanthrope indeed, in whose breast something like a jovial feeling is not roused – in whose mind some pleasant associations are not awakened – by the recurrence of Christmas. There are people who will tell you that Christmas is not to them what it used to be; that each succeeding Christmas has found some cherished hope, or happy prospect, of the year before, dimmed or passed away; that the present only serves to remind them of reduced circumstances and straightened incomes – of the feasts they once bestowed on hollow friends, and of the cold looks that meet them now, in adversity and misfortune. Never heed such dismal reminiscences. There are few men who have lived long enough in the world, who cannot call up such thoughts any day in the year. Then do not select the merriest of the three hundred and sixty-five, for your doleful recollections, but draw your chair nearer the blazing fire – fill the glass and send round the song – and if your room be smaller than it was a dozen years ago, or if your glass be filled with reeking punch, instead of sparkling wine, put a good face on the matter, and empty it off-hand, and fill another, and troll off the old ditty you used to sing, and thank God it's no worse. Look on the merry faces of your children (if you have any) as they sit round the fire. One little seat may be empty; one slight form that gladdened the father's heart, and roused the mother's pride to look upon, may not be there. Dwell not upon the past; think not that one short year ago, the fair child now resolving into dust, sat before you, with the bloom of health upon its cheek, and the gaiety of infancy in its joyous eye. Reflect upon your present blessings – of which every man has many – not on your past misfortunes, of which all men have some. Fill your glass again, with a merry face and contented heart. Our life on it, but your Christmas shall be merry, and your new year a happy one!

Who can be insensible to the outpourings of good feeling, and the honest interchange of affectionate attachment, which abound at this season of the year? A Christmas family-party! We know nothing in nature more delightful! There seems a magic in the very name of Christmas. Petty jealousies and discords are forgotten; social feelings are awakened, in bosoms to which they have long been strangers; father and son, or brother and sister, who have met and passed with averted gaze, or a look of cold recognition, for months before, proffer and return the cordial embrace, and bury their past animosities in their present happiness. Kindly hearts that have yearned towards each other, but have been withheld by false notions of pride and self-dignity, are again reunited, and all is kindness and benevolence! Would that Christmas lasted the whole year through (as it ought), and that the prejudices and passions which deform our better nature, were never called into action among those to whom they should ever be strangers!

The Christmas family-party that we

mean, is not a mere assemblage of relations, got up at a week or two's notice, originating this year, having no family precedent in the last, and not likely to be repeated in the next. No. It is an annual gathering of all the accessible members of the family, young or old, rich or poor; and all the children look forward to it, for two months beforehand, in a fever of anticipation. Formerly, it was held at grandpapa's; but grandpapa getting old, and grandmamma getting old too, and rather infirm, they have given up housekeeping, and have domesticated themselves with uncle George; so, the party always takes place at uncle George's house, but grandmamma sends in most of the good things, and grandpapa always *will* toddle down, all the way to Newgate-market, to buy the turkey, which he engages a porter to bring home behind him in triumph, always insisting on the man's being rewarded with a glass of spirits, over and above his hire, to drink "a merry Christmas and a happy new year" to aunt George. As to grandmamma, she is very secret and mysterious for two or three days beforehand, but not sufficiently so to prevent rumours getting afloat that she has purchased a beautiful new cap with pink ribbons for each of the servants, together with sundry books, and pen-knives, and pencil-cases, for the younger branches; to say nothing of divers secret additions to the order originally given by aunt George at the pastry-cook's, such as another dozen of mince-pies for the dinner, and a large plum-cake for the children.

On Christmas-eve, grandmamma is always in excellent spirits, and after employing all the children, during the day, in stoning the plums, and all that, insists, regularly every year, on uncle George coming down into the kitchen, taking off his coat, and stirring the pudding for half an hour or so, which

uncle George good-humouredly does to the vociferous delight of the children and servants. The evening concludes with a glorious game of blind-man's-buff, in an early stage of which grandpapa takes great care to be caught, in order that he may have an opportunity of displaying his dexterity.

On the following morning, the old couple, with as many of the children as the pew will hold, go to church in great state: leaving aunt George at home dusting decanters and filling castors, and uncle George carrying bottles into the dining-parlour, and calling for cork-screws, and getting into everybody's way.

When the church-party return to lunch, grandpapa produces a small sprig of misletoe from his pocket, and tempts the boys to kiss their little cousins under it – a proceeding which affords both the boys and the old gentleman unlimited satisfaction, but which rather outrages grandmamma's ideas of decorum, until grandpapa says, that when he was just thirteen years and three months old, *he* kissed grandmamma under a misletoe too, on which the children clap their hands, and laugh very heartily, as do aunt George and uncle George; and grandmamma looks pleased, and says, with a benevolent smile, that grandpapa was an impudent young dog, on which the children laugh very heartily again, and grandpapa more heartily than any of them.

But all these diversions are nothing to the subsequent excitement when grandmamma in a high cap, and slate-coloured silk gown; and grandpapa with a beautifully plaited shirt-frill, and white neckerchief; seat themselves on one side of the drawing-room fire, with uncle George's children and little cousins innumerable, seated in the front, waiting the arrival of the expected visitors. Suddenly a hackney-coach is heard to stop, and uncle George, who has been looking out of the window, exclaims "Here's Jane!" on which the children rush to the door, and helter-skelter down stairs; and uncle Robert and aunt Jane, and the dear little baby, and the nurse, and the whole party, are ushered up stairs amidst tumultuous shouts of "Oh, my!" from the children, and frequently repeated warnings not to hurt baby from the nurse. And grand-papa takes the child, and grandmamma kisses her daughter, and the confusion of this first entry has scarcely subsided, when some other aunts and uncles with more cousins arrive, and the grown-up cousins flirt with each other, and so do the little cousins too, for that matter, and nothing is to be heard but a confused din of talking, laughing, and merriment.

A hesitating double knock at the street-door, heard during a momentary pause in the conversation, excites a general inquiry of "Who's that?" and two or three children, who have been stand-ing at the window, announce in a low voice, that it's "poor aunt Margaret." Upon which, aunt George leaves the room to welcome the new comer; and grandmamma draws herself up, rather stiff and stately; for Margaret married a poor man without her consent, and poverty not being a sufficiently weighty punishment for her offence, has been discarded by her friends, and debarred the society of her dearest relatives. But Christmas has come round, and the unkind feelings that have struggled against better dispositions during the year, have melted away before its genial influence, like half-formed ice beneath the morning sun. It is not difficult in a moment of angry feeling for a parent to denounce a disobedient child; but, to banish her at a period of general good will and hilarity, from the hearth, round which she has sat on so many annivers-aries of the same day, expanding by slow degrees from infancy to girlhood, and

then bursting, almost inperceptibly into a woman, is widely different. The air of conscious rectitude, and cold forgiveness, which the old lady has assumed, sits ill upon her; and when the poor girl is led in by her sister, pale in looks and broken in hope – not from poverty, for that she could bear, but from the consciousness of undeserved neglect, and unmerited un-kindness – it is easy to see how much of it is assumed. A momentary pause suc-ceeds; the girl breaks suddenly from her sister and throws herself, sobbing, on her mother's neck. The father steps hastily forward, and takes her husband's hand. Friends crowd round to offer their hearty congratulations, and happiness and harmony again prevail.

As to the dinner, it's perfectly delight-ful – nothing goes wrong, and everybody is in the very best of spirits, and disposed to please and be pleased. Grandpapa relates a circumstantial account of the purchase of the turkey, with a slight digression relative to the purchase of previous turkeys, on former Christmas-days, which grandmamma corroborates in the minutest particular. Uncle George tells stories, and carves poultry, and takes wine, and jokes with the children at the side-table, and winks at the cousins that are making love, or being made love to, and exhilarates everybody with his good humour and hospitality; and when, at last, a stout servant, staggers in with a gigantic pudding, with a sprig of holly in the top, there is such a laughing, and shouting, and clapping of little chubby hands, and kicking up of fat dumpy legs, as can only be equalled by the applause with which the astonishing feat of pour-ing lighted brandy into mince-pies, is received by the younger visitors. Then the dessert! – and the wine! – and the fun! Such beautiful speeches, and *such* songs, from aunt Margaret's husband, who turns out to be such a nice man, and *so* attentive to grandmamma! Even grandpapa not only sings his annual song with unprecedented vigour, but on being honoured with an unanimous *encore*, according to annual custom, actually comes out with a new one which nobody but grandmamma ever heard before; and a young scape-grace of a cousin, who has been in some disgrace with the old people, for certain heinous sins of omission and commission – neglecting to call, and persisting in drinking Burton ale – astonishes everybody into convulsions of laughter by volunteering the most extraordinary comic songs that ever were heard. And thus the evening passes, in a strain of rational good-will and cheerfulness, doing more to awaken the sympathies of every member of the party in behalf of his neighbour, and to perpetuate their good feeling during the ensuing year, than half the homilies that have ever been written, by half the Divines that have ever lived.

Here comes the Christmas pudding! A 19th century scene from *Pears' Annual* of 1896; the original painting "Christmas comes but once a year" was by Charles Green.

"The Wassail Bowl" – an anonymous
19th century print.

Christmas carols – sung by the choir of Salisbury
Cathedral, Wiltshire, England.

THE CHRISTMAS CAROL

William Wordsworth

The minstrels played their Christmas
  tune
    To-night beneath my cottage eaves;
While, smitten by a lofty moon,
    The encircling laurels, thick with
      leaves,
Gave back a rich and dazzling sheen
That overpowered their natural green.

Through hill and valley every breeze
    Had sunk to rest, with folded wings:
Keen was the air, but could not freeze
    Nor check the music of the strings;
So stout and hardy were the band
That scraped the chords with strenuous
  hand!

And who but listened – till was paid
    Respect to every inmate's claim:
The greeting given, the music played,
    In honor of each household name,
Duly pronounced with lusty call,
And "Merry Christmas" wished to all!

How touching, when, at midnight, sweep
    Snow-muffled winds, and all is dark,
To hear, and sink again to sleep!
    Or, at an earlier call, to mark
By blazing fire, the still suspense
Of self-complacent innocence;

The mutual nod, – the grave disguise
    Of hearts with gladness brimming
      o'er;
And some unbidden tears that rise
    For names once heard, and heard no
      more;
Tears brightened by the serenade
For infant in the cradle laid.

Hail ancient Manners! sure defence,
    Where they survive, of wholesome
      laws;
Remnants of love whose modest sense
    Thus into narrow room withdraws;
Hail, Usages of pristine mould,
And ye that guard them, Mountains old!

"Journey through the snow" – a painting by Henry Alken.

A VISIT FROM ST. NICHOLAS

Clement C. Moore

'Twas the night before Christmas, when all through the house
Not a creature was stirring, not even a mouse;
The stockings were hung by the chimney with care,
In hopes that St. Nicholas soon would be there;
The children were nestled all snug in their beds,
While visions of sugar-plums danced through their heads;
And mamma in her kerchief, and I in my cap,
Had just settled our brains for a long winter's nap, –
When out on the lawn there arose such a clatter,
I sprang from my bed to see what was the matter.
Away to the window I flew like a flash,
Tore open the shutters and threw up the sash.
The moon, on the breast of the new-fallen snow,
Gave a lustre of midday to objects below;
When what to my wondering eyes should appear,
But a miniature sleigh and eight tiny reindeer,
With a little old driver, so lively and quick
I knew in a moment it must be St. Nick.
More rapid than eagles his courses they came,
And he whistled and shouted and called them by name;
"Now, Dasher! now, Dancer! now, Prancer and Vixen!

On, Comet! on, Cupid! on, Donder and Blitzen!
To the top of the porch, to the top of the wall!
Now, dash away, dash away, dash away all!"
As dry leaves that before the wild hurricane fly,
When they meet with an obstacle, mount to the sky,
So, up to the house-top the coursers they flew,
With a sleigh full of toys, – and St. Nicholas too.
And then in a twinkling I heard on the roof
The prancing and pawing of each little hoof,
As I drew in my head and was turning around,
Down the chimney St. Nicholas came with a bound.
He was dressed all in fur from his head to his foot,
And his clothes were all tarnished with ashes and soot;
A bundle of toys he had flung on his back,
And he looked like a pedlar just opening his pack.
His eyes how they twinkled! his dimples how merry!
His cheeks were like roses, his nose like a cherry;
His droll little mouth was drawn up like a bow,
And the beard on his chin was as white as the snow.
The stump of a pipe he held tight in his teeth,

THE SAME OLD-
FASHIONED GREETING
FROM THE SAME OLD FRIEND YOU KNOW
MAY SANTA BRING
HIS CHOICEST GIFTS
TO YOU ACROSS THE SNOW

"May Santa bring his choicest gifts . . ." – a 19th century Christmas card.

And the smoke it encircled his head like a wreath.
He had a broad face, and a little round belly
That shook, when he laughed, like a bowl full of jelly.
He was chubby and plump, – a right jolly old elf –
And I laughed when I saw him, in spite of myself.
A wink of his eye and a twist of his head
Soon gave me to know I had nothing to dread.
He spoke not a word, but went straight to his work,
And filled all the stockings; then turned with a jerk,
And laying his finger aside of his nose,
And giving a nod, up the chimney he rose.
He sprang to his sleigh, to his team gave a whistle,
And away they all flew like the down of a thistle;

But I heard him exclaim, ere he drove out of sight:
"Happy Christmas to all, and to all a good-night!"

Some children get over-excited!

THE FIR TREE

Hans Christian Andersen

OUT in the forest stood a pretty little Fir Tree. It had a good place; it could have sunlight, air there was plenty, and all around grew many larger comrades – pines as well as firs. But the little Fir Tree wished ardently to become greater. It did not care for the warm sun and the fresh air; it took no notice of the peasant children, who went about talking together, when they had come out to look for strawberries and raspberries. Often they came with a whole potfull, or had strung berries on a straw; then they would sit down by the little Fir Tree and say, "How pretty and small that one is!" and the Tree did not like to hear that at all.

Next year he had grown a great joint, and the following year he was longer still, for in fir trees one can always tell by the number of rings they have how many years they have been growing.

"Oh, if I were only as great a tree as the others!" sighed the little Fir, "then I would spread my branches far around, and look out from my crown into the wide world. The birds would then build nests in my boughs, and when the wind blew I could nod just as grandly as the others yonder."

He took no pleasure in the sunshine, in the birds, and in the red clouds that went sailing over him morning and evening.

When it was winter, and the snow lay all around, white and sparkling, a hare would often come jumping along, and spring right over the little Fir Tree. Oh! this made him so angry. But two winters went by, and when the third came the little Tree had grown so tall that the hare was obliged to run around it.

"Oh! to grow, to grow, and become old; that's the only fine thing in the world," thought the Tree.

In the autumn woodcutters always came and felled a few of the largest trees; that was done this year too, and the little Fir Tree, that was now quite well grown, shuddered with fear, for the great stately trees fell to the ground with a crash, and their branches were cut off, so that the trees looked quite naked, long, and slender – they could hardly be recognized. But then they were laid upon wagons, and horses dragged them away out of the wood. Where were they going? What destiny awaited them?

In the spring, when the swallows and the Stork came, the Tree asked them, "Do you know where they were taken? Did you not meet them?"

The swallows knew nothing about it, but the Stork looked thoughtful, nodded his head, and said,

"Yes, I think so, I met many new ships when I flew out of Egypt; on the ships were stately masts; I fancy that these were the trees. They smelt like fir. I can assure you they're stately – very stately."

"Oh that I were only big enough to go over the sea! What kind of thing is the sea, and how does it look?"

"It would take too long to explain all that," said the Stork, and he went away.

"Rejoice in thy youth," said the Sunbeams; "rejoice in thy fresh growth, and in the young life that is within thee."

And the wind kissed the Tree, and the dew wept tears upon it; but the Fir Tree did not understand that.

When Christmas-time approached, quite young trees were felled, sometimes trees which were neither so old nor so large as this Fir Tree, that never rested but always wanted to go away. These young trees, which were almost the most beautiful, kept all their branches; they were put upon wagons, and horses dragged them away out of the wood.

"Where are they all going?" asked the Fir Tree, "They are not greater than I – indeed, one of them was much smaller. Why do they keep all their branches? Whither are they taken?"

"We know that! We know that!" chirped the Sparrows. "Yonder in the town we looked in at the windows. We know where they go. Oh! they are dressed up in the greatest pomp and splendor that can be imagined. We have looked in at the windows, and have perceived that they are planted in the middle of the warm room, and adorned with the most beautiful things – gilt apples, honey-cakes, playthings, and many hundreds of candles."

"And then?" asked the Fir Tree, and trembled through all its branches. "And then? What happens then?"

"Why, we have not seen anything more. But it was incomparable."

"Perhaps I may be destined to tread this glorious path one day!" cried the Fir Tree rejoicingly. "That is even better than traveling across the sea. How painfully I long for it! If it were only Christmas now! Now I am great and grown up, like the rest who were led away last year. Oh, if I were only on the carriage! If I were only in the warm room, among all the pomp and splendor! And then? Yes, then something even better will come, something far more

charming, or else why should they adorn me so? There must be something grander, something greater still to come; but what? Oh, I'm suffering, I'm longing! I don't know myself what is the matter with me!"

"Rejoice in us," said Air and Sunshine. "Rejoice in thy fresh youth here in the woodland."

But the Fir Tree did not rejoice at all, but it grew and grew; winter and summer it stood there, green, dark green. The people who saw it said, "That's a handsome tree!" and at Christmas-time it was felled before any one of the others. The axe cut deep into its marrow, and the tree fell to the ground with a sigh: it felt a pain, a sensation of faintness, and could not think at all of happiness, for it was sad at parting from its home, from the place where it had grown up: it knew that it should never again see the dear old companions, the little bushes and flowers all around – perhaps not even the birds. The parting was not at all agreeable.

The Tree only came to itself when it was unloaded in a yard, with other trees, and heard a man say,

"This one is famous; we only want this one!"

Now two servants came in gay liveries, and carried the Fir Tree into a large beautiful saloon. All around the walls hung pictures, and by the great stove stood large Chinese vases with lions on the covers; there were rocking-chairs, silken sofas, great tables covered with picture-books, and toys worth a hundred times a hundred dollars, at least the children said so. And the Fir Tree was put into a great tub filled with sand; but no one could see that it was a tub, for it was hung round with green cloth, and stood on a large many-colored carpet. Oh, how the Tree trembled! What was to happen now? The servants, and the young ladies also, decked it out. On one

The Victorian Christmas tree. A painting by Viggo Johansen (1851–1935).

branch they hung little nets, cut out of colored paper; every net was filled with sweetmeats; golden apples and walnuts hung down as if they grew there, and more than a hundred little candles, red, white, and blue, were fastened to the different boughs. Dolls that looked exactly like real people – the Tree had never seen such before – swung among the foliage, and high on the summit of the Tree was fixed a tinsel star. It was splendid, particularly splendid.

"This evening," said all, "this evening it will shine."

"Oh," thought the Tree, "that it were evening already! Oh that the lights may be soon lit up! When may that be done? I wonder if trees will come out of the forest to look at me? Will the sparrows fly against the panes? Shall I grow fast here, and stand adorned in summer and winter?"

Yes, he did not guess badly. But he had a complete backache from mere longing, and the backache is just as bad for a Tree as the headache for a person.

At last the candles were lighted. What a brilliance, what splendor! The Tree trembled so in all its branches that one of the candles set fire to a green twig, and it was scorched.

"Heaven preserve us!" cried the young ladies; and they hastily put the fire out.

Now the Tree might not even tremble. Oh, that was terrible! It was so afraid of setting fire to some of its ormaments, and it was quite bewildered with all the brilliance. And now the folding doors were thrown open, and a number of children rushed in as if they would have overturned the whole Tree; the older people followed more deliberately. The little ones stood quite silent, but only for a minute; then they shouted till the room rang; they danced gleefully round the Tree, and one present after another was plucked from it.

"What are they about?" laughed the Tree. "What's going to be done?"

And the candles burned down to the twigs, and as they burned down they were extinguished, and then the children received permission to plunder the Tree. Oh! they rushed in upon it, so that every branch cracked again: if it had not been fastened by the top and by the golden star to the ceiling, it would have fallen down.

The children danced about with their pretty toys. No one looked at the Tree except one old man, who came up and peeped among the branches, but only to see if a fig or an apple had not been forgotten.

"A story! a story!" shouted the children: and they drew a little fat man towards the Tree; and he sat down just beneath it, – "for then we shall be in the green wood," said he, "and the tree may have the advantage of listening to my tale. But I can only tell one. Will you hear the story of Ivede-Avede, or of Klumpey-Dumpey, who fell down stairs, and still was raised up to honor and married the Princess?"

"Ivede-Avede!" cried some, "Klumpey-Dumpey!" cried others, and there was a great crying and shouting. Only the Fir Tree was quite silent, and thought, "Shall I not be in it? shall I have nothing to do in it?" But he had been in the evening's amusement, and had done what was required of him.

And the fat man told about Klumpey-Dumpey, who fell down stairs, and yet was raised to honor and married the Princess. And the children clapped their hands, and cried, "Tell another! tell another!" for they wanted to hear about Ivede-Avede; but they only got the story of Klumpey-Dumpey. The Fir Tree stood quite silent and thoughtful; never had the birds in the wood told such a story as that. Klumpey-Dumpey fell down stairs, and yet came to honor and married the Princess!

"Yes, so it happens in the world!" thought the Fir Tree, and believed it must be true, because that was such a nice man who told it. "Well, who can know? Perhaps I shall fall down stairs too, and marry a Princess!" And it looked forward with pleasure to being adorned again, the next evening, with candles and toys, gold and fruit. "To-morrow I shall not tremble," it thought. "I will rejoice in all my splendor. To-morrow I shall hear the story of Klumpey-Dumpey again, and, perhaps, that of Ivede-Avede too."

And the Tree stood all night quiet and thoughtful.

In the morning the servants and the chambermaid came in.

"Now my splendor will begin afresh," thought the Tree. But they dragged him out of the room, and up stairs to the garret, and here they put him in a dark corner where no daylight shone.

"What's the meaning of this?" thought the Tree. "What am I to do here? What is to happen?"

And he leaned against the wall, and thought, and thought. And he had time enough, for days and nights went by, and nobody came up; and when at length some one came, it was only to put some great boxes in a corner. Now the Tree stood quite hidden away, and the supposition was that it was quite forgotten.

"Now it's winter outside," thought the Tree. "The earth is hard and covered with snow, and people cannot plant me; therefore I suppose I'm to be sheltered here until spring comes. How considerate that is! How good people are! If it were only not so dark here, and so terribly solitary! – not even a little hare! That was pretty out there in the wood, when the snow lay thick and the hare sprang past; yes, even when he jumped over me; but

then I did not like it. It is terribly lonely up here!"

"Piep! piep!" said a little Mouse, and crept forward, and then came another little one. They smelt at the Fir Tree, and then slipped among the branches.

"It's horribly cold," said the two little Mice, "or else it would be comfortable here. Don't you think so, you old Fir Tree?"

"I'm not old at all," said the Fir Tree. "There are many much older than I."

"Where do you come from?" asked the Mice. "And what do you know?" They were dreadfully inquisitive. "Tell us about the most beautiful spot on earth. Have you been there? Have you been in the store-room, where cheeses lie on the shelves, and hams hang from the ceiling, where one dances on tallow candles, and goes in thin and comes out fat?"

"I don't know that!" replied the Tree; "but I know the wood, where the sun shines, and where the birds sing."

And then it told all about its youth.

And the little Mice had never heard anything of the kind; and they listened and said,

"What a number of things you have seen! How happy you must have been!"

"I?" said the Fir Tree; and it thought about what it had told. "Yes, those were really quite happy times." But then he told of the Christmas-eve, when he had been hung with sweetmeats and candles.

"Oh!" said the little Mice, "how happy you have been, you old Fir Tree!"

"I'm not old at all," said the Tree. "I only came out of the wood this winter. I'm only rather backward in my growth."

"What splendid stories you can tell!" said the little Mice.

And next night they came with four other little Mice, to hear what the Tree had to relate; and the more it said, the more clearly did it remember everything, and thought, "Those were quite merry days! But they may come again. Klumpey-Dumpey fell down stairs, and yet he married the Princess. Perhaps I may marry a Princess too!" And then the Fir Tree thought of a pretty little birch tree that grew out in the forest: for the Fir Tree, that birch was a real Princess.

"Who's Klumpey-Dumpey?" asked the little Mice.

And then the Fir Tree told the whole story. It could remember every single word: and the little Mice were ready to leap to the very top of the tree with pleasure. Next night a great many more Mice came, and on Sunday two Rats even appeared; but these thought the story was not pretty, and the little Mice were sorry for that, for now they also did not like it so much as before.

"Do you only know one story?" asked the Rats.

"Only that one," replied the Tree. "I heard that on the happiest evening of my life; I did not think then how happy I was."

"That's a very miserable story. Don't you know any about bacon and tallow candles – a store-room story?"

"No," said the Tree.

"Then we'd rather not hear you," said the Rats.

And they went back to their own people. The little Mice at last stayed away also; and then the Tree sighed and said,

"It was very nice when they sat round me, the merry little Mice, and listened when I spoke to them. Now that's past too. But I shall remember to be pleased when they take me out."

But when did that happen? Why, it was one morning that people came and rummaged in the garret: the boxes were put away, and the Tree brought out; they certainly threw him rather roughly on the floor, but a servant dragged him away at once to the stairs, where daylight shone.

"Now life is beginning again," thought the Tree.

It felt the fresh air and the first sunbeams, and now it was out in the courtyard. Everything passed so quickly that the Tree quite forgot to look at itself, there was so much to look at all round. The courtyard was close to the garden, and here everything was blooming; the roses hung fresh and fragrant over the little paling, the linden trees were in blossom, and the swallows cried, "Quinze-wit! quinze-wit! my husband's come!" But it was not the Fir Tree that they meant.

"Now I shall live!" said the Tree, rejoicingly, and spread its branches far out; but, alas! they were all withered and yellow; and it lay in the corner among nettles and weeds. The tinsel star was still upon it, and shone in the bright sunshine.

In the courtyard a couple of the merry children were playing, who had danced round the tree at Christmas-time, and had rejoiced over it. One of the youngest ran up and tore off the golden star.

"Look what is sticking to the ugly old fir tree," said the child, and he trod upon the branches till they cracked again under his boots.

And the Tree looked at all the blooming flowers and the splendor of the garden, and then looked at itself, and wished it had remained in the dark corner of the garret; it thought of its fresh youth in the wood, of the merry Christmas-eve, and of the little Mice which had listened so pleasantly to the story of Klumpey-Dumpey.

"Past! past!" said the old Tree. "Had I but rejoiced when I could have done so! Past! past!"

And the servant came and chopped the Tree into little pieces; a whole bundle lay there, it blazed brightly under the great brewing copper, and it sighed deeply, and each sigh was like a little shot: and the children who were at play there ran up and seated themselves at the fire, looked into it, and cried, "Puff! puff!" But at each explosion, which was a deep sigh, the Tree thought of a summer day in the woods, or of a winter night there, when the stars beamed; he thought of Christmas-eve and of Klumpey-Dumpey, the only story he had ever heard or knew how to tell; and then the Tree was burned.

The boys played in the garden, and the youngest had on his breast a golden star, which the Tree had worn on its happiest evening. Now that was past, and the Tree's life was past, and the story is past too: past! past! – and that's the way with all stories.

"The Christmas Tree" by Ditz.

A CHRISTMAS CAROL

Christina G. Rossetti

In the bleak mid-winter
    Frosty wind made moan,
Earth stood hard as iron,
    Water like a stone;
Snow had fallen, snow on snow,
    Snow on snow,
In the bleak mid-winter
    Long ago.

Our God, Heaven cannot hold him
    Nor earth sustain;
Heaven and earth shall flee away,
    When he comes to reign.
In the bleak mid-winter
    A stable-place sufficed
The Lord God Almighty,
    Jesus Christ.

Angels and archangels
    May have gathered there;
Cherubim and seraphim
    Thronged the air.
But only His Mother,
    In her maiden bliss,
Worshipped her Beloved
    With a kiss.

What can I give Him,
    Poor as I am?
If I were a shepherd
    I would bring a lamb;
If I were a wise man,
    I would do my part, –
Yet what I can I give Him,
    Give my heart.

Winter scene by Antoni Van Verstralen (1594–1641).

SONG OF THE HOLLY

William Shakespeare

Blow, blow thou winter wind –
  Thou art not so unkind
    As man's ingratitude!
  Thy tooth is not so keen,
  Because thou art not seen,
    Although thy breath be rude.
Heigh ho! sing heigh ho! unto the green
  holly:
Most friendship is feigning, most loving
  mere folly.
  Then heigh ho! the holly!
  This life is most jolly!

Freeze, freeze, though bitter sky –
  Thou dost not bite so nigh
    As benefits forgot!
  Though thou the waters warp,
  Thy sting is not so sharp
    As friend remembered not.
Heigh ho! sing heigh ho! unto the green
  holly:
Most friendship is feigning, most loving
  mere folly.
  Then heigh ho! the holly!
  This life is most jolly!

Bringing in the Yule Log in New England.

Gathering holly in the Pennines, England:
a painting by Gertrude Halsband.

CHRISTMAS TODAY

Part pagan, part Christian and hallowed by tradition, Christmas is the festival when families gather together, exchange presents, spoil children and eat too much. Every family has its own way of organizing Christmas Day and its own set of rituals, but the true Christmas today revolves around three: the Church, Christmas dinner and presents.

In the western world, Christmas is the celebration of the birth of Jesus Christ, and traditionally it is the time of year when all Christians go to church either to Midnight Mass or to services on Christmas Day itself. If there are small children in the family, there will be a deputation to church on Christmas morning to sing carols and Christmas hymns while the cook is left alone in the kitchen to prepare the Christmas dinner. Then, church over, impatience barely concealed, everyone will tear home to start opening presents or to enjoy those that have already been delivered by Santa Claus.

In grown-up families there are many who eat their main Christmas meal in the evening, but for the majority with children it is the midday meal, featuring turkey, plum pudding, crackers to pull and funny paper hats to wear. Again, the other crucial decision is *when* to open the main presents. Is it to be after breakfast, before breakfast, before lunch or after lunch? Every family will have its own time for opening, but there is much to be said for splitting the present opening into two sessions – before lunch, when the cook's main work is complete and the family can gather around the Christmas tree for a drink, and after lunch, when crackers have been pulled and everyone has paper hats on their heads.

However, amid all the excitement and festivity, various tasks have to be carried out. First, lists must be kept so that everyone knows who has given what to whom so that 'thank you' letters may be sent. Somebody has to gather up the waste paper for burning or disposal; someone else must organize the kitchen and washing up. When presents are open and stowed away, some families will go out for the traditional Christmas walk, visit friends and relatives, or simply relax by the fire.

Everyone has their own idea of the perfect Christmas. Some take extravagant holidays in the sun, others spend the season helping the poor or the elderly; those who are working are happy to snatch a few blissful moments of celebration in the midst of a busy routine. For most people the ideal Christmas is little different from that of the nineteenth century – the delight of children, a warm fire, a sparkling Christmas tree, a tasty dinner, a wealth of presents and a great deal of Christmas cheer.

Christmas in New York: a giant ribbon adorns one of the big stores.

YOUR OWN SPECIAL CHRISTMAS DECORATIONS

Making your own Christmas decorations can be much more fun than just buying ready-made ones from the stores. All you need are scissors, glue, a pencil, plenty of colored paper – and a little imagination. Here are some ideas. There are many variations on these themes, and lots of ways to embellish them – tinsel and gold or silver dust can be added to give extra sparkle to your designs; and colors can be mixed to make bright and seasonal effects.

SIMPLE PAPER CHAIN

1   Cut strips of colored paper about eight inches by half- or three-quarters of an inch.

2   Take one of the strips; glue one end and stick the other end to it, to form a ring. This makes the first link in our chain.

3   Loop another colored strip through this first one and glue the ends together. Continue looping and glueing to make a chain as long as you like.

All sorts of colors looks best: you can even cut up pages from color magazines to add variety of color within the individual links of the chain.

1

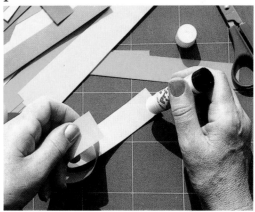

2

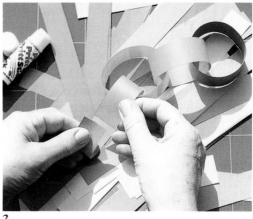

3

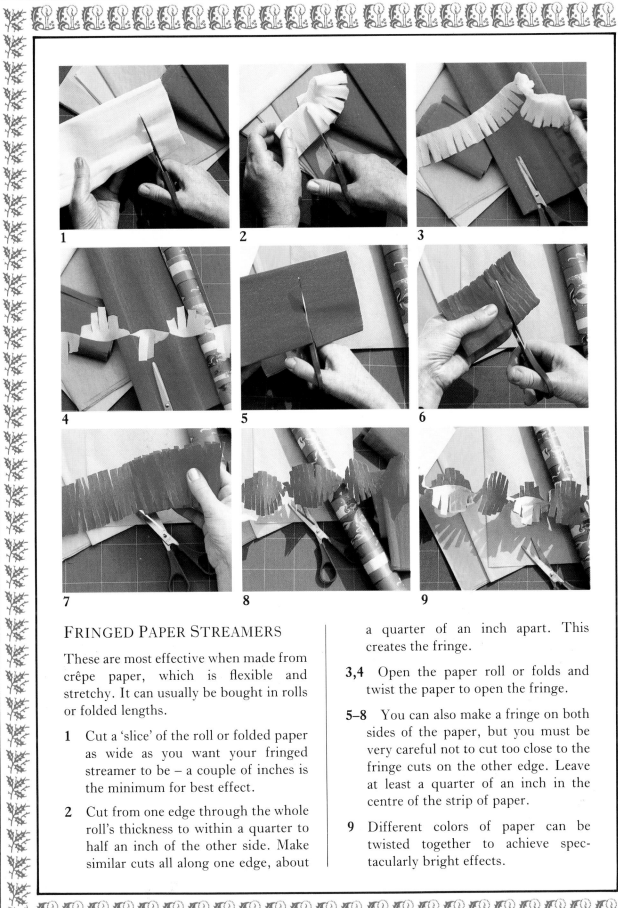

1

2

3

4

5

6

7

8

9

FRINGED PAPER STREAMERS

These are most effective when made from crêpe paper, which is flexible and stretchy. It can usually be bought in rolls or folded lengths.

1 Cut a 'slice' of the roll or folded paper as wide as you want your fringed streamer to be – a couple of inches is the minimum for best effect.

2 Cut from one edge through the whole roll's thickness to within a quarter to half an inch of the other side. Make similar cuts all along one edge, about a quarter of an inch apart. This creates the fringe.

3,4 Open the paper roll or folds and twist the paper to open the fringe.

5–8 You can also make a fringe on both sides of the paper, but you must be very careful not to cut too close to the fringe cuts on the other edge. Leave at least a quarter of an inch in the centre of the strip of paper.

9 Different colors of paper can be twisted together to achieve spectacularly bright effects.

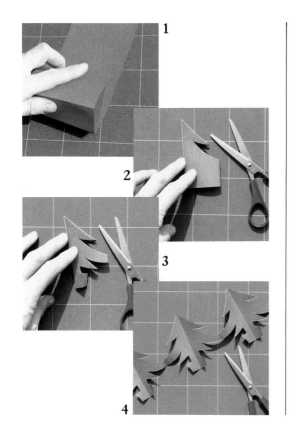

REPEAT PATTERNS – ROWS OF CHRISTMAS TREES

1 Cut your paper four or five inches deep by as wide as you like or the paper will allow. Fold into one-and-a-half to two inches wide.

2 Cut from one edge of the paper the pattern you want duplicated – in the example illustrated we have chosen a Christmas tree motif. It is easier to make a symmetrical pattern this way. Be sure to cut through all the layers of the folded paper at the same time.

3 Cut the pattern, but be sure to leave at least one point on the cut edge uncut, so that you have a 'hinge' at the fold in order to hold the repeating pattern together.

4 Open out the folded image and you will find not only the whole tree but lots of them, all joined together.

REPEAT PATTERNS – CHRISTMAS FAIRIES

1 Draw the silhouette of a fairy on a piece of thin card as in the illustration; the height of the fairy here is five inches, but you can make these to any scale you like, according to the size of paper you have. You can also draw other characters and shapes, but you must always allow parts of the design to stretch out opposite each other so that the repeating pattern can be linked at the folds of the paper. In this case, the fairies will be holding hands. Cut around the outline of the fairy on the cardboard to make yourself a template.

2 Cut a strip of paper as long as you want your row of fairies and as deep as the fairy template you have just cut out.

3 Fold the paper to the same width as the extended arms of fairy template. The number of folds you make will determine the number of fairies in your chain.

4,5 Place the template on top of the folded paper and trace around it on to the paper.

6,7 Cut the paper – all the layers at the same time – to the outline of the fairy, remembering not to cut the folded edges at the ends of the fairy's arms, for here they will be holding hands.

8,9 Unfold the paper and you will have a row of fairies.

You can draw any shape or character you like and repeat it in this way – a star, for

1   2   3

4   5   6

7   8   9

example, joining the opposite points; or angels with big wings joined tip to tip. The important thing to remember is not to cut the hinge edges – or the row of shapes will fall to pieces.

All sorts of papers and colors can be used – pages from color magazines, for example. You can decorate the patterns with silver and gold dust sprinkled on to a glued surface; you can add eyes and a mouth to the fairies or angels; and you can cut discs of gold paper to stick behind the angels heads, just showing around the top, to look like haloes.

THE CHRISTMAS STOCKING

The magic of Christmas is embodied in the visit of Santa Claus. Children all over the world hang up their stockings or pillows on Christmas Eve and go to bed, over-excited and tense, awaiting the arrival of Santa and his reindeer. You wake once and he hasn't come. You wake a second time and he hasn't come. You wake a third time and he still hasn't come. But on the fourth time . . . there, he has been. The stocking that was empty is now full, lights are switched on, brothers and sisters are woken and presents are torn open and gloated over with the wrapping paper strewn around the bedroom. Everyone can remember those magic moments.

The story of Santa Claus and the custom of giving gifts at Christmas both stem from ancient times. The original Santa Claus was St Nicholas of Myra who lived during the 4th century. He was a miracle worker who gave all his money to the poor; one legend claims that he brought three boys back to life who had been murdered by a cruel butcher and stored as pickled meat in a barrel. They were revived by his love, faith and prayer.

In another legend St. Nicholas found an impoverished nobleman with three beautiful daughters who were unable to wed because their father had gambled away all his fortune and was unable to provide them with a dowry. St. Nicholas heard this story and saw the stockings of the three girls hanging up to dry by the fire, so he filled them with bags of gold coins which he threw down the chimney. This legend is the origin of all the stockings that are hung up by chimneys and at the end of beds the whole world over.

In some countries, children put out their shoes. In France children put them out on the hearth, while in Holland they are filled with hay and carrots for Santa Claus's white horse. Santa Claus then places his presents in the shoes. In some houses, gifts of food, mince pies and glasses of ale or sherry are placed out for Santa on the mantle shelf to fortify him as he slides back up the chimney, and every household will have their own tradition.

There are certain important rules to observe. The first is that some weeks before Christmas each child must write a letter to Santa Claus asking for those presents that they particularly want. The letters have to be shown to the parents and then, where possible, burnt and posted in the form of ashes up the chimney. These ashes fly all the way to Santa Claus Land in Greenland where they descend onto the white snow and become once again legible.

All parents, all Father Christmasses, know the intense pleasure and difficulty of fulfilling the role of Santa Claus to perfection. There are certain practical considerations. The first and most important is to have wrapping paper specially kept aside for the Christmas stocking which does not appear on any other present and is hidden carefully away from all children. The second is to get a good selection of small gifts with one or two larger ones, all of which can be neatly fitted into the stocking together with oranges or tangerines, some chocolate buttons and possibly a coin or two. Gifts to avoid are musical instruments, which may wake the whole household rather earlier than anybody wishes, nasty surprises like furry spiders, and too many chocolates, which may all be eaten before breakfast. Then, in the morning, stocking opened, the presents can be brought to the parents' bedroom. Everyone can delight in the age-old generosity of Santa and the never-failing joy of Christmas.

A homely scene from today's Christmas. Christmas cards are hung to add to the other decorations; the tree sparkles with all sorts of pretty things; and gifts wait to be unwrapped.

CHRISTMAS FOOD AND DRINK

Of all the festivals, Christmas is the easiest on the cook; the menu is fixed long in advance, hallowed by tradition and eagerly anticipated by everyone.

Traditionally, the roast for Christmas day used to be goose – the turkeys that nowadays grace most tables are a comparatively recent arrival. But whether your choice is turkey or goose, Christmas dinner generally follows the same pattern: a starter of smoked salmon, potted shrimps or clear soup, followed by heaped plates of roast turkey with all the trimmings, and finally by Christmas pudding and brandy butter or sauce. For children, the Chistmas pudding can be replaced with ice cream and fruit salad (which may prove to be more popular) and afterwards nuts, crystalized fruit, or the traditional Stilton cheese of England – if anyone has room for another mouthful. Christmas is a time for overeating.

ROAST TURKEY

The size of the bird you choose is largely determined by the number of people you are going to feed (and also how fond you are of eating cold turkey for the next few days). Once you have bought your turkey, the next thing to do is to stuff it. This should be done at least twelve hours before the bird is cooked, and the important thing about stuffing recipes is that they should be moist and contain enough fat to counteract the natural dryness of the bird itself. When the stuffing has been completed, wrap the turkey in two layers of kitchen foil and put the bird in an oven preheated to gas mark 8 or 445°F; after 15 minutes reduce the oven temperature to gas mark 5 or 380°F and allow 20–25 minutes for each *pound* of the turkey weighed, as prepared for the oven but before stuffing. Half an hour before the cooking is complete, remove the top layers of foil to let the turkey brown.

TRADITIONAL TURKEY STUFFINGS
Chestnut and Sausage-meat Stuffing
   1lb chestnuts
   1¾lb sausage meat
   Whisky
   Seasoning
Peel the chestnuts of both skins. The easiest way to do this is to cut a ring around the top. Put the chestnuts in cold water and then bring this to the boil for 1 minute. Remove and then pull off the skins with the help of a knife: this is a task all the family can help with, including the children. Then, cook the chestnuts in stock, preferably made with the giblets of the turkey, until tender. This usually takes about 30 minutes to ¾ of an hour. Fold them into the sausage meat. Add ¾ tbs. of whisky. Season with salt and pepper.

Walnut Stuffing
   ½lb veal
   ½lb lean pork
   Liver and heart of the turkey
   ¼lb (1c) chopped walnuts
   2 tbs brandy
   Salt
   Pepper

"Dinner is served" – the Christmas dinner table in a typical American
household today.

Herbs

Mince all the meats together and pound them until they are well blended. Add roughly chopped nuts, brandy, parsley, thyme and seasoning.

Mushroom Stuffing
- Turkey liver
- 3–4 chicken livers
- 2 rashers bacon
- ¾lb mushrooms
- 4oz (1c) fresh breadcrumbs
- 2 small onions
- 1 clove garlic
- Salt
- Pepper
- Parsley
- 2 eggs

Chop the bacon and liver finely. Slice the mushrooms and sauté in butter until tender. Then mix them with the liver and bacon. Chop the two onions finely and mix everything together. Add two eggs to bind the mixture.

Prune and Apple Stuffing
- 2½oz (½c) boiled rice
- 4 sweet apples
- 18 prunes
- Liver of the turkey
- Stick of celery
- Grated peel of half a small lemon
- Salt
- Pepper
- Ground mace
- Parsley
- 1 egg
- 2 ounces butter

Soak the prunes overnight and then cook them. Cut them in half and remove the stones. Chop the celery. Peel, core and slice the apples. Then combine all the ingredients and add the beaten egg last of all.

Accompaniments
To accompany the roast turkey, it is traditional to have roast or mashed potatoes – it is much easier to have mashed potatoes as if you attempt to have roast potatoes you will have an oven clash – plus brussel sprouts with chestnuts. When peeling the chestnuts for the chestnut and sausage-meat stuffing, the best thing to do is to double or triple the quantity and cook them all at the same time. Then put the ones not used for the stuffing on one side and add them to the brussel sprouts when these are cooked the following day.

CHRISTMAS PUDDING

The vast majority of Christmas puddings are bought ready-made. They then only have to be steamed and the brandy sauce or brandy butter added. For housewives who wish to make their own Christmas pudding, here is a traditional recipe. It must be made in September and can be kept for as long as 15 months (i.e., eaten the following Christmas). This presupposes that you have perfect storing conditions, cool and dry.

- 1lb (8½c) fresh white breadcrumbs
- 4oz (1c) flour
- 1lb (2c) fresh chopped suet
- 2oz (⅓c) freshly grated coconut
- 1½lb (3c) stoned raisins
- 1lb (3⅓c) currants
- 1lb (3c) sultanas
- ½lb (1½c) mixed candied peel
- 3oz (¾c) almonds
- Grated peel of a lemon and orange
- ½lb (1½c) Demerara sugar
- Grated nutmeg
- 2 sherry glasses (½c) of brandy or
- 4 glasses (1c) if the pudding is for next year
- 1 pint (2½c) barley wine
- 6 eggs
- 2 tbs black treacle
- 1 grated carrot

Mix all the dry ingredients together and stir-in the beaten eggs one at a time and then the treacle. Add the barley wine and finally the brandy. Put the mixture into well-greased basins in which a round of buttered greaseproof paper has been laid on the base. Fill each base about three quarters full and press the mixture well down to eliminate any air bubbles. Cover with two or more rounds of greaseproof paper and tie it down with a square of linen. Then steam the puddings for between six and ten hours according to the size of the basin. Allow the puddings to cool and the cloths to dry before storing them. On Christmas Day they will need only another two to four hours of steaming. If you plan to keep the puddings until the following year, replace the wet cloths immediately with dry ones; inspect the puddings once or twice during the year, and if there is any sign of mould remove the greaseproof paper, scrape away the mouldy pudding, put on new rounds of paper soaked in cognac and a new sterilized pudding cloth.

Brandy Butter
- 1lb (2c) unsalted butter
- 1lb (3c) icing sugar
- Brandy to taste

Cream the butter and then add the sugar. When these are well mixed together add brandy to taste.

Brandy Sauce
- ½oz flour
- ½ (1⅕c) pint milk
- knob of butter
- 1 tbs sugar
- 1–2 tbs brandy

Melt the butter in a saucepan and add the flour to make a smooth paste. Add the milk and bring to the boil, stirring constantly; add brandy to taste.

The classic Christmas pudding with brandy ablaze.

CHRISTMAS DRINKS

Christmas is the traditional time of year when mulled wine, lambswool, rum punch, mulled ale and eggnog are all dispensed. If you are planning to serve one of these drinks, the imporant things to remember are: first, have the drink hot; second, have good, thick, strong glasses that do not crack; third and most important, have a scrupulously clean pan made of enamel or stainless steel – you must never use copper, iron or brass utensils when making drinks containing wine or beer.

Cheap Mulled Wine
   One bottle cheap red wine
   2½ tbs brandy
   5 fluid oz water
   10–12 lumps sugar
   2 oranges
   4 allspice berries
   4 cloves
   1 small stick of cinnamon
Rub the sugar vigorously on the outside of the oranges and then put it in the pan with water and spices. Bring to the boil and then leave to simmer for 5 minutes. Add the wine, brandy, the juice of one orange and the remaining orange cut into horizontal slices. Heat slowly until the wine is too hot to put your finger into but is still below boiling point. Do remember that boiling evaporates off the alcohol and rob these drinks of their potency.

Rum Punch
   ⅔ pint (2c) tea (freshly made and
      stood for only 3 minutes)
   ½ pint (1¼c) orange juice
   6 tbs lemon juice
   8 tbs (½c) white sugar
   ½ pint (1¼c) rum
   2 tbs Cointreau

Pour the hot tea over the sugar and stir until it dissolves. Then add the fruit juices and bring back almost to boiling point. Add the rum and Cointreau and raise the heat again, but do not boil.

Mulled Ale

Bring 1 pint (2½c) of mild beer nearly to boiling point and season with grated nutmeg and a pinch each of powdered allspice, ginger, cinnamon and a touch of coriander. Add a strip of lemon peel and 1 tbs of Demerara sugar. Just before serving, add a port-glass of brandy.

Lambswool (to make 12 glasses)
    1 pint (20fl oz) of beer
    ¾ pint (15fl oz) dry white wine
    6 tbs brown sugar
    Seasoning of cinnamon, ginger and
        nutmeg
    4 small apples

Bake the apples in the oven until they are cooked and the flesh fluffs up. Heat the ale and wine together, and stir in the sugar and spices. Put the cooked apples through a sieve and dilute the pulp with a little of the hot ale before stirring it into the main body of the liquid. Bring it all back to boiling point and serve immediately.

Eggnog
    6 separated eggs
    4oz (½c) white sugar
    ½ pint (1¼c) of double cream
    ½ pint (1¼c) of milk
    1–2 tbs sherry, brandy or rum
    2 tsp of vanilla or rum extract
    Grated nutmeg

Beat the egg whites in a bowl until they are stiff but not dry, and gradually add the sugar. Beat the yolks in another bowl until they are lemon yellow. Fold in the egg whites. In a third bowl beat the cream until it is stiff, then add to the egg along with the milk and other ingredients. Chill. Sprinkle with grated nutmeg before serving. Note that the eggnog may need a gentle stir before being served.

THE SPIRIT
OF CHRISTMAS

Charles Dickens

And numerous indeed are the hearts to which Christmas brings a brief season of happiness and enjoyment. How many families whose members have been dispersed and scattered far and wide, in the restless struggles of life, and are then re-united, and meet once again in that happy state of companionship and mutual good-will, which is a source of such pure and unalloyed delight, and one so incompatible with the cares and sorrows of the world, that the religious belief of the most civilized nations, and the rude traditions of the roughest savages, alike number it among the first joys of a future state of existence, provided for the blest and happy! How many old recollections, and how many dormant sympathies, does Christmas time awaken!

We write these words now, many miles distant from the spot at which, year after year, we met on that day, a merry and joyous circle. Many of the hearts that throb so gaily then, have ceased to beat; many of the looks that shone so brightly then, have ceased to glow; the hands we grasped, have grown cold; the eyes we sought, have hid their lustre in the grave; and yet the old house, the room, the merry voices and smiling faces, the jest, the laugh, the most minute and trivial circumstance connected with those happy meetings, crowd upon our mind at each recurrence of the season, as if the last assemblage had been but yesterday. Happy, happy Christmas, that can win us back to the delusions of our childish days, that can recall to the old man the pleasures of his youth, and transport the sailor and the traveler, thousands of miles away, back to his own fireside and his quiet home!

Snowflakes in New York City: spectacular Christmas decorations at the junction of 58th and 5th Avenue.

The Christmas tree in Trafalgar Square, London, England.